WHAT'S THE BIG IDEA?

NOTES & DETAILS

ACTION ITEMS

THINK OUTSIDE THE BOX!

ACTIONS

PROS

IDEA

CONS

NOTES

WORK
BACKWARD

END RESULT

ALMOST THERE . . .

BACKTRACK EVEN FURTHER . . .

WHAT'S NEXT . . .

BEFORE THAT

FIRST STEP

IDEA

MIND MAP

1

2

3

4

5

6

7

8

9

10

SOLVE A PROBLEM

PROBLEM

SOLUTION

PROBLEM

SOLUTION

PROBLEM

SOLUTION

BRAIN DUMP

+ =

+ =

+ =

+ =

+ =

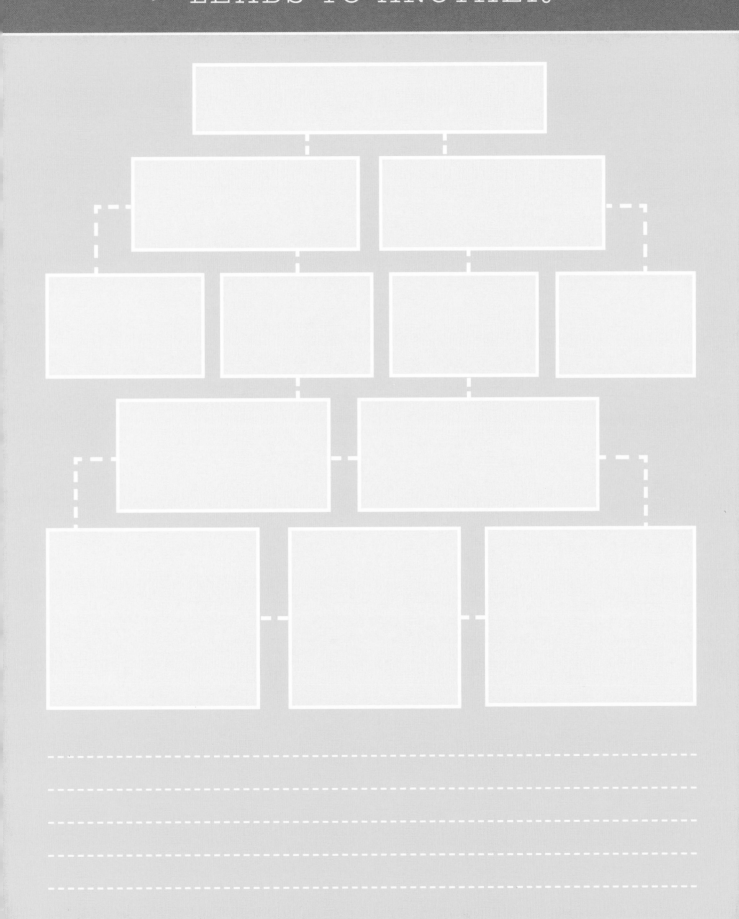

IDEA FUNNEL

IDEA

NARROW IT DOWN

TIGHTEN IT UP

MAKE IT CLEAR

JUST THE FACTS

ONE-SENTENCE CONCEPT

TOPIC YOU WANT TO EXPLORE

EVERY CRAZY IDEA THAT COMES TO MIND:

>>> PICK ONE IDEA

STEPS TO EXECUTE:

- [ ] _____
- [ ] _____
- [ ] _____
- [ ] _____
- [ ] _____
- [ ] _____
- [ ] _____

- [ ] _____
- [ ] _____
- [ ] _____
- [ ] _____
- [ ] _____
- [ ] _____

IT WOULD BE GREAT IF:

THINGS WOULD BE EASIER IF:

WHAT I CAN DO ABOUT IT:

WHAT'S THE BIG IDEA?

NOTES & DETAILS

ACTION ITEMS

ACTIONS

PROS

IDEA

CONS

NOTES

WORK
BACKWARD

END RESULT

ALMOST THERE . . .

BACKTRACK EVEN FURTHER . . .

WHAT'S NEXT . . .

BEFORE THAT

FIRST STEP

IDEA

MIND MAP

1

2

3

4

5

6

7

8

9

10

SOLVE A PROBLEM

PROBLEM

SOLUTION

PROBLEM

SOLUTION

PROBLEM

SOLUTION

BRAIN DUMP

+ =

+ =

+ =

+ =

+ =

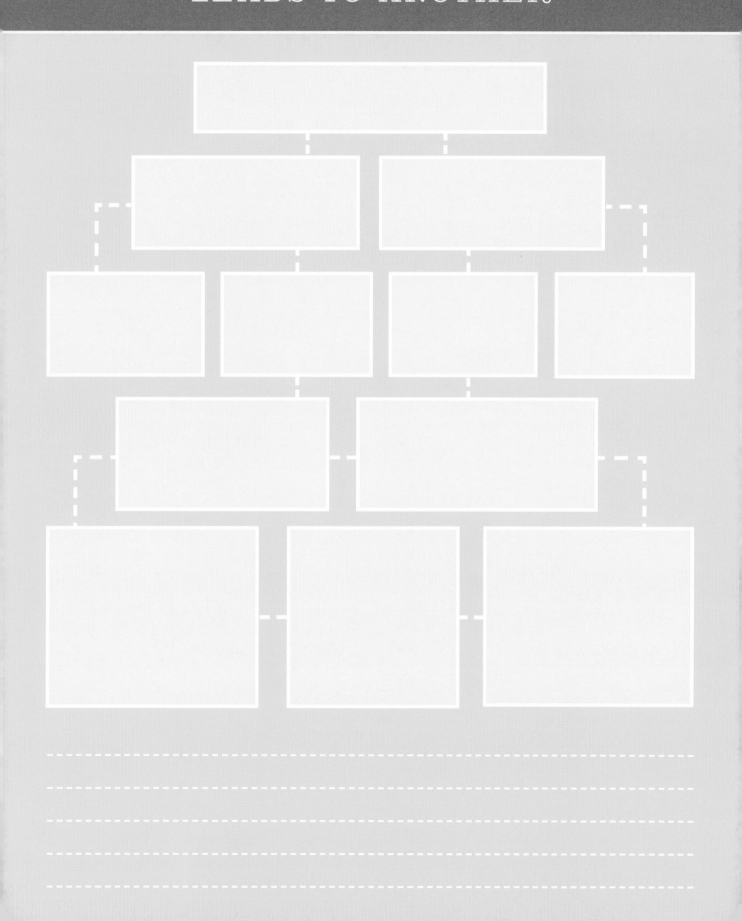

IDEA FUNNEL

IDEA

NARROW IT DOWN

TIGHTEN IT UP

MAKE IT CLEAR

JUST THE FACTS

ONE-SENTENCE CONCEPT

TOPIC YOU WANT TO EXPLORE

EVERY CRAZY IDEA THAT COMES TO MIND:

>>> PICK ONE IDEA

STEPS TO EXECUTE:

- [ ] _____
- [ ] _____
- [ ] _____
- [ ] _____
- [ ] _____
- [ ] _____
- [ ] _____

- [ ] _____
- [ ] _____
- [ ] _____
- [ ] _____
- [ ] _____
- [ ] _____
- [ ] _____

IT WOULD BE GREAT IF:

THINGS WOULD BE EASIER IF:

WHAT I CAN DO ABOUT IT:

WHAT'S THE BIG IDEA?

NOTES & DETAILS

ACTION ITEMS

THINK OUTSIDE THE BOX!

ACTIONS

PROS

IDEA

CONS

NOTES

WORK
BACKWARD

END RESULT

ALMOST THERE . . .

BACKTRACK EVEN FURTHER . . .

WHAT'S NEXT . . .

BEFORE THAT

FIRST STEP

IDEA

MIND MAP

1

2

3

4

5

6

7

8

9

10

SOLVE A PROBLEM

PROBLEM

SOLUTION

PROBLEM

SOLUTION

PROBLEM

SOLUTION

BRAIN DUMP

+   =

+   =

+   =

+   =

+   =

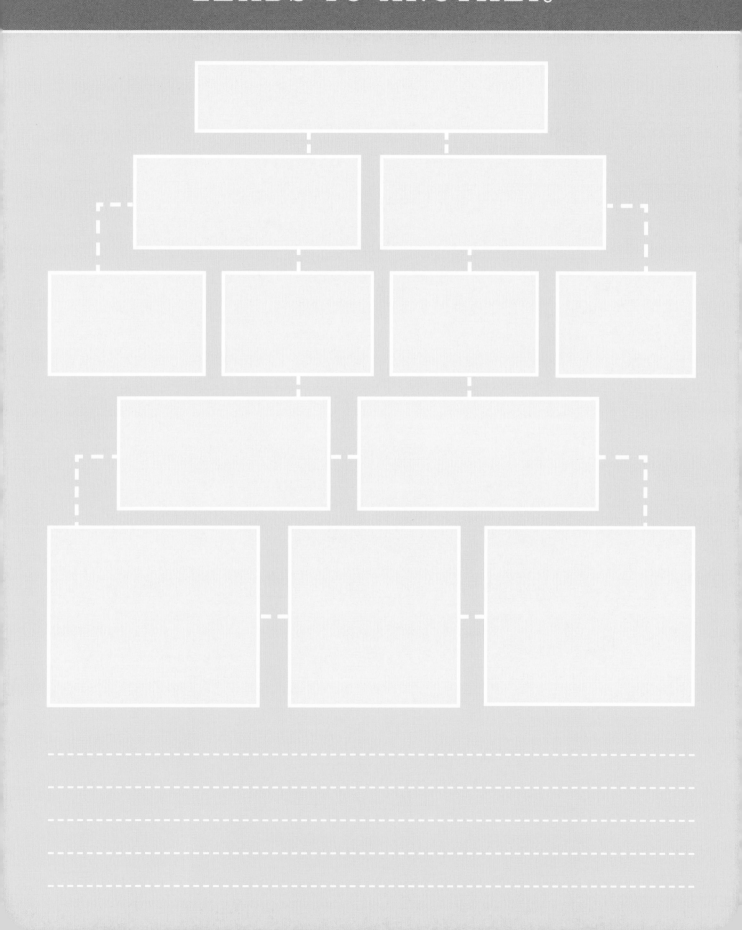

IDEA FUNNEL

IDEA

NARROW IT DOWN

TIGHTEN IT UP

MAKE IT CLEAR

JUST THE FACTS

ONE-SENTENCE CONCEPT

TOPIC YOU WANT TO EXPLORE

EVERY CRAZY IDEA THAT COMES TO MIND:

>>> PICK ONE IDEA

STEPS TO EXECUTE:

- [ ] _____
- [ ] _____
- [ ] _____
- [ ] _____
- [ ] _____
- [ ] _____
- [ ] _____

- [ ] _____
- [ ] _____
- [ ] _____
- [ ] _____
- [ ] _____
- [ ] _____

IT WOULD BE GREAT IF:

THINGS WOULD BE EASIER IF:

WHAT I CAN DO ABOUT IT:

WHAT'S the BIG IDEA?

NOTES & DETAILS

ACTION ITEMS

THINK OUTSIDE THE BOX!

ACTIONS

PROS

IDEA

CONS

NOTES

WORK
BACKWARD

END RESULT

ALMOST THERE . . .

BACKTRACK EVEN FURTHER . . .

WHAT'S NEXT . . .

BEFORE THAT

FIRST STEP

IDEA

1

2

3

4

5

6

7

8

9

10

SOLVE A PROBLEM

PROBLEM

SOLUTION

PROBLEM

SOLUTION

PROBLEM

SOLUTION

BRAIN DUMP

\+   =

\+   =

\+   =

\+   =

\+   =

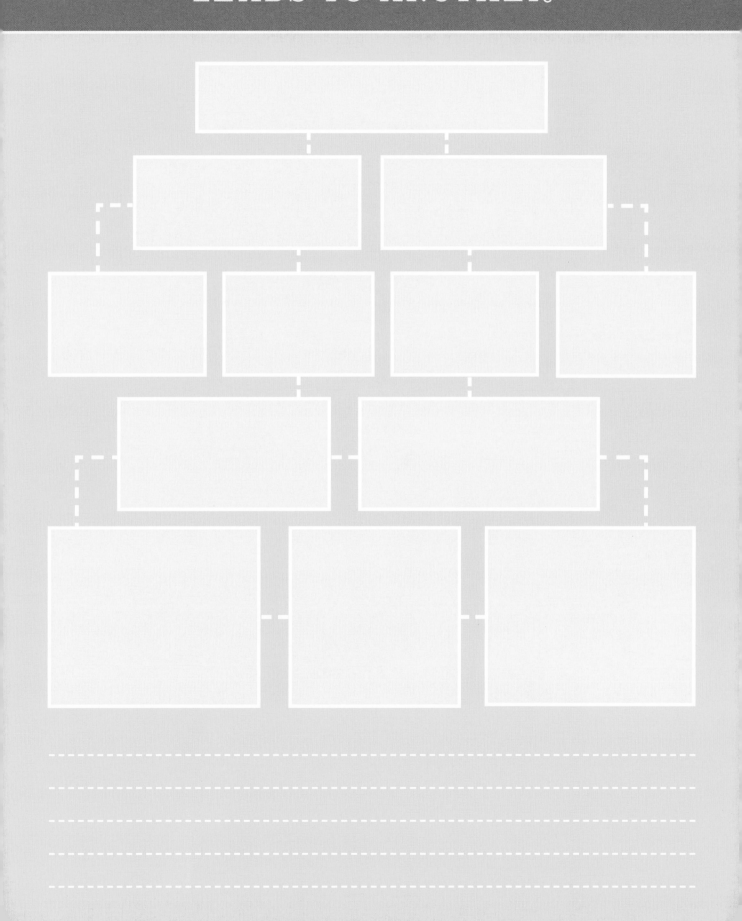

IDEA FUNNEL

IDEA

NARROW IT DOWN

TIGHTEN IT UP

MAKE IT CLEAR

JUST THE FACTS

ONE-SENTENCE CONCEPT

TOPIC YOU WANT TO EXPLORE

EVERY CRAZY IDEA THAT COMES TO MIND:

>>> PICK ONE IDEA

STEPS TO EXECUTE:

- [ ] _____
- [ ] _____
- [ ] _____
- [ ] _____
- [ ] _____
- [ ] _____
- [ ] _____

- [ ] _____
- [ ] _____
- [ ] _____
- [ ] _____
- [ ] _____
- [ ] _____
- [ ] _____

IT WOULD BE GREAT IF:

THINGS WOULD BE EASIER IF:

WHAT I CAN DO ABOUT IT:

WHAT'S the BIG IDEA?

NOTES & DETAILS

ACTION ITEMS

THINK OUTSIDE THE BOX!

ACTIONS

PROS

IDEA

CONS

NOTES

WORK
BACKWARD

END RESULT

ALMOST THERE . . .

BACKTRACK EVEN FURTHER . . .

WHAT'S NEXT . . .

BEFORE THAT

FIRST STEP

IDEA

MIND MAP

1

2

3

4

5

6

7

8

9

10

SOLVE A PROBLEM

PROBLEM

SOLUTION

PROBLEM

SOLUTION

PROBLEM

SOLUTION

BRAIN DUMP

+   =

+   =

+   =

+   =

+   =

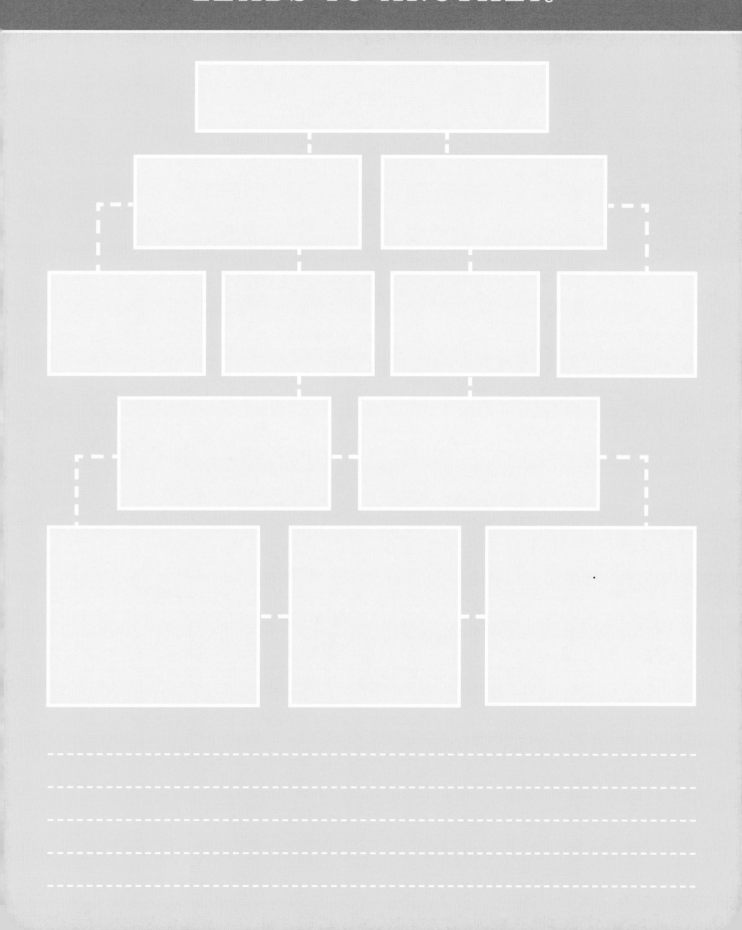

IDEA FUNNEL

IDEA

NARROW IT DOWN

TIGHTEN IT UP

MAKE IT CLEAR

JUST THE FACTS

ONE-SENTENCE CONCEPT

TOPIC YOU WANT TO EXPLORE

EVERY CRAZY IDEA THAT COMES TO MIND:

>>> PICK ONE IDEA

STEPS TO EXECUTE:

- [ ] _____
- [ ] _____
- [ ] _____
- [ ] _____
- [ ] _____
- [ ] _____
- [ ] _____

- [ ] _____
- [ ] _____
- [ ] _____
- [ ] _____
- [ ] _____
- [ ] _____
- [ ] _____

IT WOULD BE GREAT IF:

THINGS WOULD BE EASIER IF:

WHAT I CAN DO ABOUT IT:

WHAT'S THE BIG IDEA?

NOTES & DETAILS

ACTION ITEMS

THINK OUTSIDE THE BOX!

ACTIONS

PROS

IDEA

CONS

NOTES

WORK
BACKWARD

END RESULT

ALMOST THERE . . .

BACKTRACK EVEN FURTHER . . .

WHAT'S NEXT . . .

BEFORE THAT

FIRST STEP

IDEA

MIND MAP

1
2
3
4
5
6
7
8
9
10

SOLVE A PROBLEM

PROBLEM

SOLUTION

PROBLEM

SOLUTION

PROBLEM

SOLUTION

BRAIN DUMP

+   =

+   =

+   =

+   =

+   =

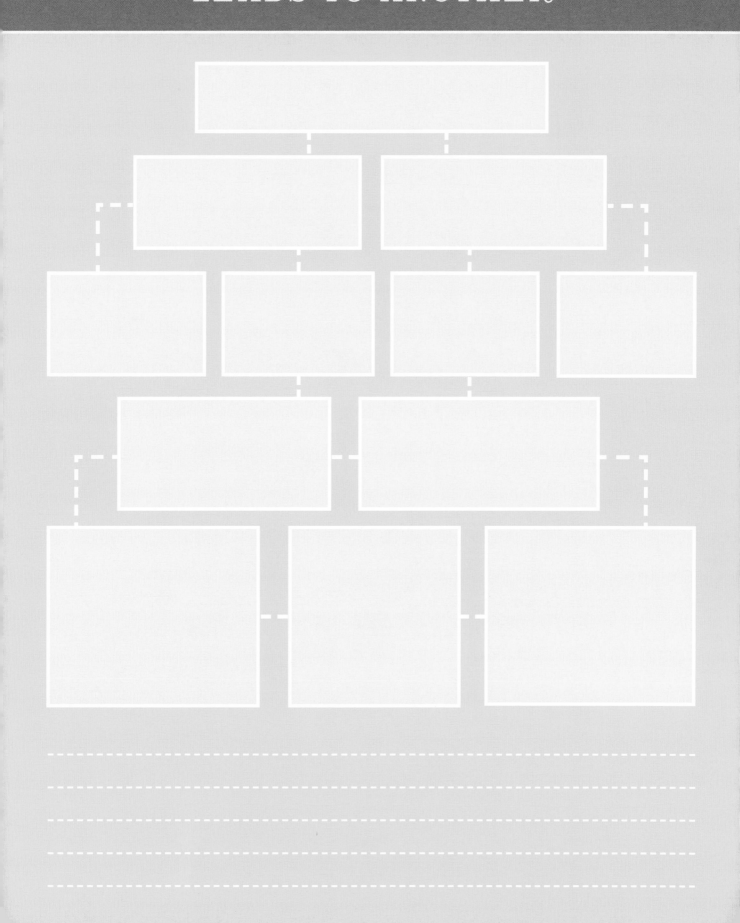

ONE IDEA
LEADS TO ANOTHER

IDEA FUNNEL

IDEA

NARROW IT DOWN

TIGHTEN IT UP

MAKE IT CLEAR

JUST THE FACTS

ONE-SENTENCE CONCEPT

TOPIC YOU WANT TO EXPLORE

EVERY CRAZY IDEA THAT COMES TO MIND:

>>> PICK ONE IDEA

STEPS TO EXECUTE:

- [ ] _____
- [ ] _____
- [ ] _____
- [ ] _____
- [ ] _____
- [ ] _____
- [ ] _____

- [ ] _____
- [ ] _____
- [ ] _____
- [ ] _____
- [ ] _____
- [ ] _____
- [ ] _____

IT WOULD BE GREAT IF:

THINGS WOULD BE EASIER IF:

WHAT I CAN DO ABOUT IT:

WHAT'S THE BIG IDEA?

NOTES & DETAILS

ACTION ITEMS

THINK OUTSIDE THE BOX!

ACTIONS

PROS

IDEA

CONS

NOTES

WORK
BACKWARD

END RESULT

ALMOST THERE . . .

BACKTRACK EVEN FURTHER . . .

WHAT'S NEXT . . .

BEFORE THAT

FIRST STEP

IDEA

MIND MAP

1

2

3

4

5

6

7

8

9

10

SOLVE A PROBLEM

PROBLEM

SOLUTION

PROBLEM

SOLUTION

PROBLEM

SOLUTION

BRAIN DUMP

I'M THINKING ABOUT

+ =

+ =

+ =

+ =

+ =

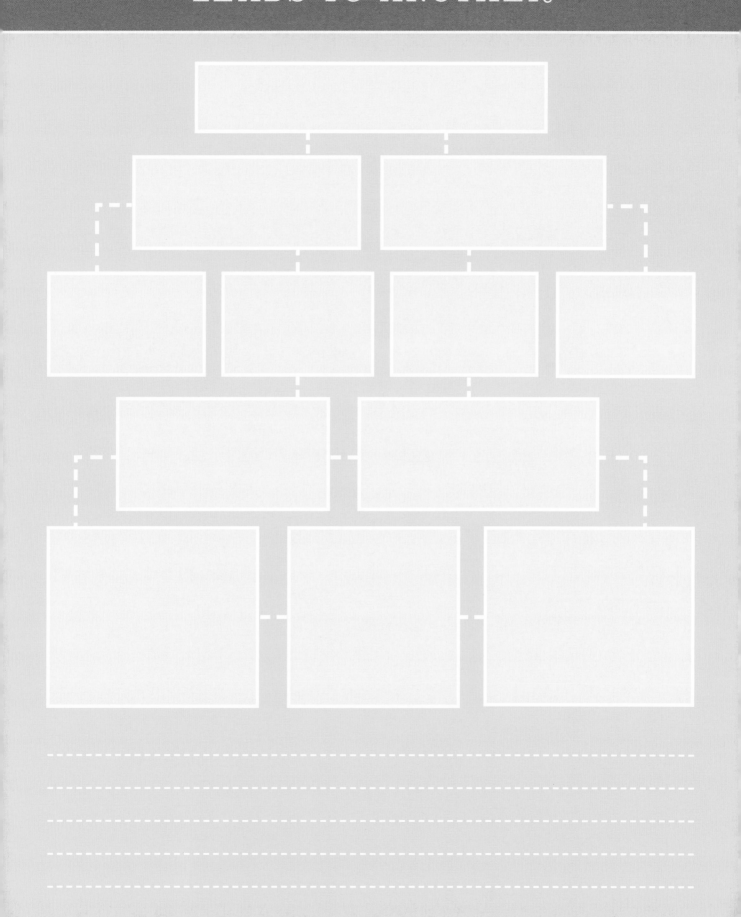

IDEA FUNNEL

IDEA

NARROW IT DOWN

TIGHTEN IT UP

MAKE IT CLEAR

JUST THE FACTS

ONE-SENTENCE CONCEPT

TOPIC YOU WANT TO EXPLORE

EVERY CRAZY IDEA THAT COMES TO MIND:

>>> PICK ONE IDEA

STEPS TO EXECUTE:

- [ ] _____
- [ ] _____
- [ ] _____
- [ ] _____
- [ ] _____
- [ ] _____
- [ ] _____

- [ ] _____
- [ ] _____
- [ ] _____
- [ ] _____
- [ ] _____
- [ ] _____
- [ ] _____

IT WOULD BE GREAT IF:

THINGS WOULD BE EASIER IF:

WHAT I CAN DO ABOUT IT:

WHAT'S THE BIG IDEA?

NOTES & DETAILS

ACTION ITEMS

THINK OUTSIDE THE BOX!

ACTIONS

PROS

IDEA

CONS

NOTES

WORK
BACKWARD

END RESULT

ALMOST THERE . . .

BACKTRACK EVEN FURTHER . . .

WHAT'S NEXT . . .

BEFORE THAT

FIRST STEP

IDEA

1

2

3

4

5

6

7

8

9

10

SOLVE A PROBLEM

PROBLEM

SOLUTION

PROBLEM

SOLUTION

PROBLEM

SOLUTION

BRAIN DUMP

+   =

+   =

+   =

+   =

+   =

ONE IDEA
LEADS TO ANOTHER

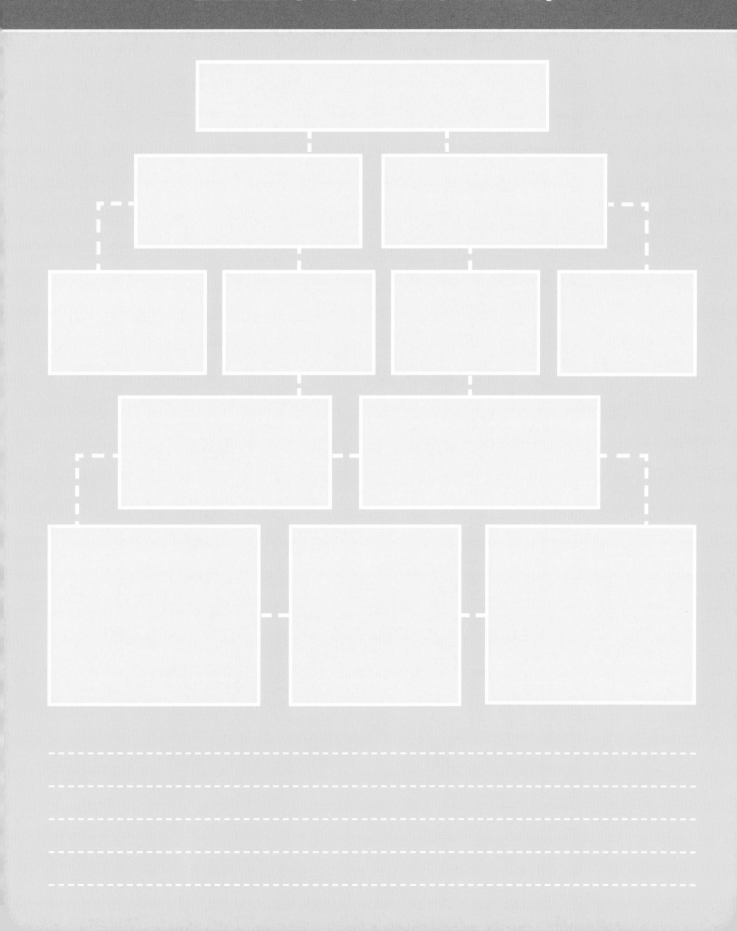

IDEA FUNNEL

IDEA

NARROW IT DOWN

TIGHTEN IT UP

MAKE IT CLEAR

JUST THE FACTS

ONE-SENTENCE CONCEPT

TOPIC YOU WANT TO EXPLORE

EVERY CRAZY IDEA THAT COMES TO MIND:

>>> PICK ONE IDEA

STEPS TO EXECUTE:

- [ ] _____
- [ ] _____
- [ ] _____
- [ ] _____
- [ ] _____
- [ ] _____
- [ ] _____

- [ ] _____
- [ ] _____
- [ ] _____
- [ ] _____
- [ ] _____
- [ ] _____
- [ ] _____

IT WOULD BE GREAT IF:

THINGS WOULD BE EASIER IF:

WHAT I CAN DO ABOUT IT:

WHAT'S the BIG IDEA?

NOTES & DETAILS

ACTION ITEMS

BIG IDEA?

THINK OUTSIDE THE BOX!

ACTIONS

PROS

IDEA

CONS

NOTES

WORK
BACKWARD

END RESULT

ALMOST THERE . . .

BACKTRACK EVEN FURTHER . . .

WHAT'S NEXT . . .

BEFORE THAT

FIRST STEP

IDEA

1
2
3
4
5
6
7
8
9
10

SOLVE A PROBLEM

PROBLEM

SOLUTION

PROBLEM

SOLUTION

PROBLEM

SOLUTION

BRAIN DUMP

+ =

+ =

+ =

+ =

+ =

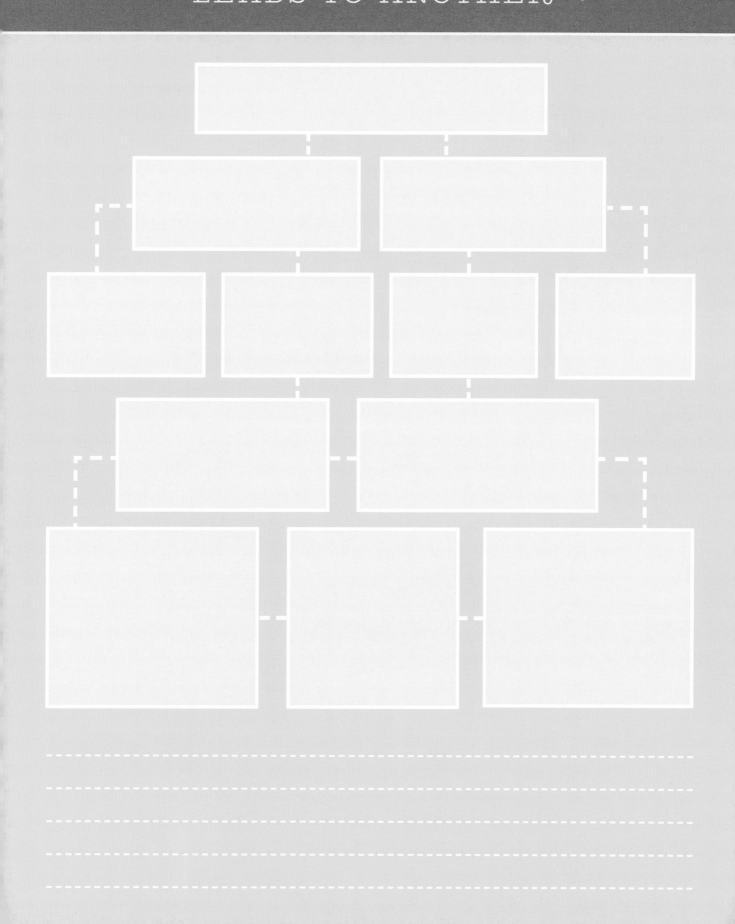

IDEA FUNNEL

IDEA

NARROW IT DOWN

TIGHTEN IT UP

MAKE IT CLEAR

JUST THE FACTS

ONE-SENTENCE CONCEPT

TOPIC YOU WANT TO EXPLORE

EVERY CRAZY IDEA THAT COMES TO MIND:

>>> PICK ONE IDEA

STEPS TO EXECUTE:

- [ ] _____
- [ ] _____
- [ ] _____
- [ ] _____
- [ ] _____
- [ ] _____
- [ ] _____

- [ ] _____
- [ ] _____
- [ ] _____
- [ ] _____
- [ ] _____
- [ ] _____
- [ ] _____

IT WOULD BE GREAT IF:

THINGS WOULD BE EASIER IF:

WHAT I CAN DO ABOUT IT: